Everything you need to know about
FROGS

AND OTHER SLIPPERY CREATURES

DK PUBLISHING

LONDON, NEW YORK, MUNICH,
MELBOURNE, and DELHI

Senior editor Carrie Love
Senior designer Claire Patané
Design Hedi Hunter and Rosie Levine
Editorial Holly Beaumont, Fleur Star,
Ben Morgan, and Alexander Cox
US editor Margaret Parrish

Consultant Brian Groombridge

Publishing manager Bridget Giles
Art director Martin Wilson
Creative director Jane Bull
Category publisher Mary Ling
Production editor Clare McLean
Production controller Claire Pearson
Picture researcher Rob Nunn
Proofreaders Caroline Stamps and
Lorrie Mack
Jacket editor Matilda Gollon

First published in the United States in 2011
by DK Publishing
1450 Broadway, Suite 801, New York, NY 10018

23 24
025–179459–Aug/2011

Copyright © 2011 Dorling Kindersley Limited

A catalog record for this book
is available from the Library of Congress.

ISBN: 978-0-7566-8232-3

Printed and bound in China

**Discover more at
www.dk.com**

Can you
SEE ME?
**This high-casqued
chameleon** (*Chamaeleo
hoehnelii*) is superb at blending in
with its surroundings. Find out
more about camouflage
on page 17.

CONTENTS

How does a fer-de-lance snake kill its prey? Discover its tactic on **page 39**.

Ribbit,

scuttle,

Which lizard is an insectivore? Take a look at **page 46**.

Why is the male midwife toad a hands-on father? See for yourself on **page 25**.

How can you survive an attack from a crocodile or alligator? Read and REMEMBER the tips on **page 71**.

How far can a leatherback sea turtle travel? Take a journey with one on **pages 60–61**.

Try to outstare a frog on **pages 30–31**. One frog will always win, since it has a spot that looks like an eye!

How does a reptile obtain heat from its surroundings? Get a glimpse on **page 28**.

slither

Play a game of snakes and ladders on **pages 50–51**. Be careful, or you might slip down an inland taipan!

When a frog sheds its skin what does it do with it? Discover the answer on **page 13**.

Amphibians

Amphibians are animals that live PARTLY in *water* and PARTLY on land. **Frogs**, toads, NEWTS, and salamanders are all **amphibians**. REPTILES have dry, *scaly skin*, but AMPHIBIANS have **soft**, moist skin. Most amphibians can breathe **through their skin**, but only if it stays *damp*. Adult amphibians can also BREATHE through lungs.

HOW MANY?
There are about **6,800** species of amphibian, most of which are *frogs*. There are about **600** species of newt and *salamander*.

Frog spawn

Most *amphibians* breed in **water**. Unlike reptiles, which lay **tough-shelled eggs** on **land**, most amphibians lay *soft, jellylike eggs* in **water**.

Is a toad a frog?

I have dry, lumpy skin that looks like it's covered in warts. People usually call me a toad, but I'm really a frog.

I'm a tree frog

Most frogs live near a **river or pools of water.** But in **rainforests, *it is so humid*** the trees are **wet** all the time, allowing some frogs to stay in them permanently. They are called *tree frogs* and have **huge, sticky fingers** to help them climb.

Most baby amphibians live entirely in **water.** Called **tadpoles,** they **swim like fish** and ***breathe through gills.*** As they grow up, they develop legs and crawl onto land, but they must always be in wet places.

Tadpoles

When a **tadpole** hatches out of an egg, its first task in life is to ***eat what's left of its egg,*** which is **full of nutrients.** In most amphibians, the tadpole changes into an adult by a process called **metamorphosis**.

Reptiles

Today, there are more than 9,000 reptile *species* on Earth; the major groups are **alligators** and *crocodiles,* TURTLES, **lizards**, and *snakes.* ALL REPTILES are **cold-blooded,** which is why they WARM THEMSELVES in *the sun* and have bodies covered in **dry,** HORNY SCALES. Some reptiles lay eggs; others give birth to live young.

HOW MANY?

Lizards make up the largest group of reptiles (with 5,461 species), followed by snakes (3,315 species), then turtles (317 species). There are fewer amphisbaenians (181 species), and even fewer crocodilians (24 species). The smallest group is the tuataras (with just 2 species).

Brightly colored

Iguanas and their relatives make up some of the most colorful of all lizards. This green iguana is brightly colored with a few markings.

All reptiles have backbones

Bright lines

The red markings on a Madagascan giant day gecko vary between individuals.

Reptiles vary greatly in *shape* and *size*. However, *all reptiles* have **scales** in contrast to the **smooth**, moist skin of amphibians. Scales differ among species, but they are a defining *feature* of a reptile.

Legless and long

Snakes are legless reptiles. They're found all over the world, but they don't do well in cold places. The Common boa constrictor, such as the one shown here, can grow to 3–13 ft (1–4 m)!

Light like sand

Like many geckos, this Sandstone gecko is colored to blend in with its surroundings.

Tuataras are a group of **reptile** found only in **New Zealand.**

What's inside?

FROGS **have simple skeletons** with fewer bones than other *vertebrates* (animals with backbones). They tend to have robust bodies and strong hind limbs. Most frogs have protruding eyes and no tail. Take a look at what's under a frog's skin.

Skull

Frogs tend to have broad heads with large sockets for the eyes. They usually have short spines and no ribs.

The hands and fingers of frogs vary according to lifestyle. Climbing frogs need fingers that can grip well.

Hand

Heart **CHAMBERS**

Frogs have a developed nervous system that is made up of a brain, nerves, and a spinal cord. A frog's heart has three chambers, whereas a mammal's has four.

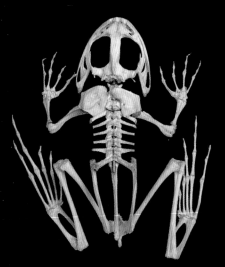

A frog's brain is structured in a similar way to a human's brain. The cerebellum (region on the top of the brain) controls posture and muscular coordination.

Elongated ankle bone

Toe bone

A frog's bone structue helps it jump a long way. The *tibia* (shin bone) and *fibula* (calf bone) are fused into a single, strong bone.

The legs and feet of frogs vary depending on where they live. Frogs that live in water have webbed toes. The more time they spend in water, the more webbed their toes are.

SNAKES have incredibly LONG necks. The neck takes up one-third of their length. Their **organs** are also long and fit in *one behind the other.* The heart is encased in a sac, but it's not fixed in place, preventing damage when swallowing a large animal.

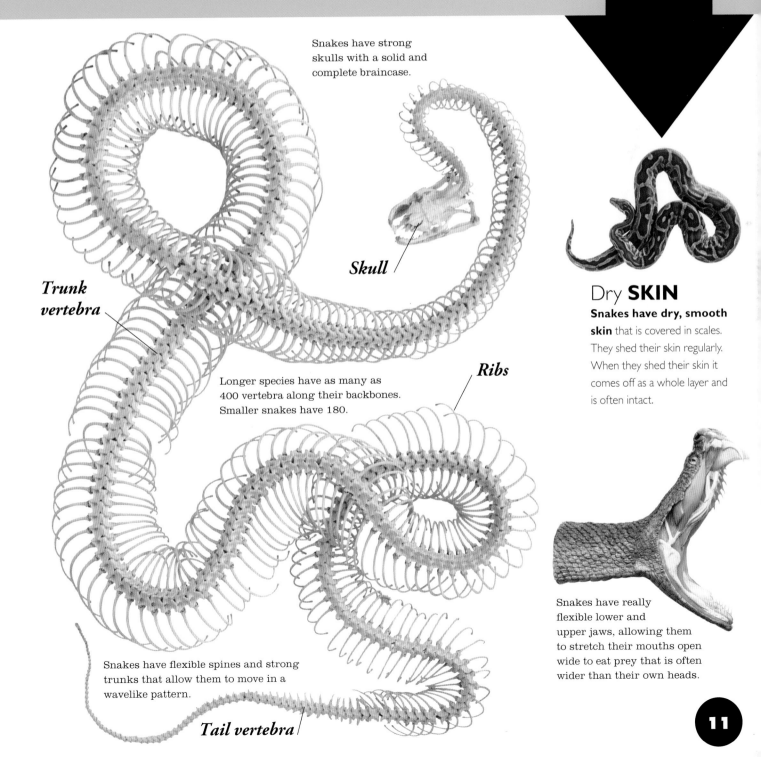

Snakes have strong skulls with a solid and complete braincase.

Skull

Trunk vertebra

Longer species have as many as 400 vertebra along their backbones. Smaller snakes have 180.

Ribs

Snakes have flexible spines and strong trunks that allow them to move in a wavelike pattern.

Tail vertebra

Dry **SKIN**
Snakes have dry, smooth skin that is covered in scales. They shed their skin regularly. When they shed their skin it comes off as a whole layer and is often intact.

Snakes have really flexible lower and upper jaws, allowing them to stretch their mouths open wide to eat prey that is often wider than their own heads.

SUPER

Frogs have very **special skin.** They don't just

FROGS don't usually SWALLOW *water* like we do. Instead, they absorb most of the **moisture** they need through *their skin*. They also get water from prey that they eat. Their skin is used to get **extra oxygen** from the water (in addition to the oxygen that's come into their lungs via their mouth cavity).

Because frogs only get OXYGEN through their skin when it's moist, they need to take GOOD CARE of it or they might suffocate. Some frogs are **slimy.** This is because their SKIN SECRETES a **mucus** that stops it from getting dry.

SKIN

wear it, they also **drink** and **breathe** through it!

Frogs regularly shed their outermost layer of skin cells to keep it healthy. This looks **pretty yucky.** They start to *twist and turn* and act like they have the **hiccups.** They do this to *stretch* out of their old skin! Finally, they **pull the skin OFF** over their head LIKE A SWEATER, and then *(this is gross)* they EAT IT! **Eeeeewww!**

Life cycle of a frog

From a baby tadpole to a young frog

Life begins

A male and a female frog come together to **mate**. Eggs are laid in *clumps* or strings. An egg *hatches* about **six days** after it's been fertilised. At first it feeds on the remains of the yolk.

Tiny tadpoles

When an egg hatches, a **tadpole's** mouth, tail, and external gills are not fully developed. At about **seven to 10 days**, a tadpole begins to **feed on algae** and attaches itself to weeds.

Fully formed

Between **12 to 16 weeks** a frog has completed its *growth cycle.* The timing varies between species and on the food and water supply. A fully formed frog starts the process afresh by mating.

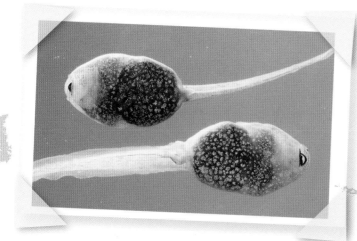

Getting bigger

At **four weeks** the *external gills* are covered by body skin. They eventually disappear and are replaced with lungs. Tadpoles have *tiny teeth* that help them to chew away at plants and algae-covered surfaces.

A bit of both

Tiny legs start to form from **six to nine weeks**. The head becomes more obvious. The *arms begin to come out*, with the elbows showing first. After **nine weeks** the tadpole is beginning to look more like a frog.

Nearly there!

By **12 weeks** the young froglet only has a small stub of a *tail*. It looks like a smaller version of an adult frog. Soon it will leave the water to live on the ground.

COLORS and

MARKINGS

AMPHIBIANS and REPTILES have a variety of *markings* and **colors.** The spectrum ranges from bright reds and blues to muddy *greens* and BROWNS. Some have **spots,** while others have *stripes*.

Texas coral snake

Markings can be deceptive! Milk snakes have thin black bands, and thick yellow and red bands. They aren't poisonous, but they appear to be dangerous because their banding is so similar to venomous **coral snakes.**

Fire salamander

Red-eyed tree frog

Regal ring-neck snake

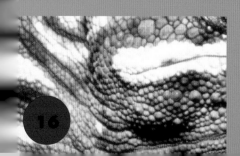

16

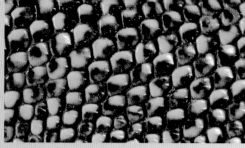

Southern dwarf chameleon

Colorful **CAMOUFLAGE**

The pattern and color of an amphibian or reptile can help it to blend in with its surroundings to hide from predators. Chameleons, as their name suggests, have an amazing ability to hide themselves by changing their appearance. They can alter their color as well as their markings.

Strawberry poison-dart frogs are bright red. This acts to warn other creatures that their skin secretions are highly toxic.

Collared lizard

Hide and seek

The Pacific tree frog is able to blend into its surroundings very easily. It reacts to seasonal changes and can switch its coloring from brown to green. It can also change its markings and the lightness of its skin according to the shift in background brightness.

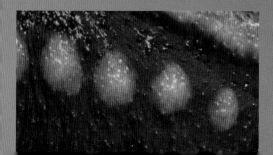

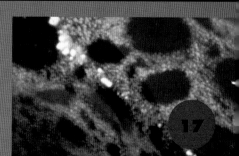

Home, Sweet Home

Amphibians are found on all continents except Antarctica. Nearly all amphibians live in or near wet areas such as streams, rivers, ponds, lakes, and other wetlands, but some display amazing adaptations that allow them to live in dry, dusty deserts. Many adult amphibians spend their lives on land, but nearly all need to lay their eggs in water.

Desert LIVING

The **desert tortoise** (*Gopherus agassizii*) spends about 95 percent of its life underground. It can go a year without water.

Couch's spadefoot toad (*Scaphiopus couchii*) gets its name from its feet, which help it to dig down through loose sand. It lives underground during dry months.

The **sandfish** (*Scincus scincus*) lives in Africa's Sahara desert and is famous for its ability to "swim" through sand.

Plant LIFE

The female **strawberry poison-dart frog** (*Oophaga pumilio*) lays her eggs on a leaf. When the tadpoles hatch, she moves them to a water-filled location.

The **gold frog** (*Brachycephalus didactylus*) makes its home in mountain rainforests. It mainly lives among leaf litter. It is a ground-dweller, since it can't jump or climb very well. The female lays eggs that hatch directly into small frogs, missing out the tadpole stage.

Up in the TREES

The **red-eyed tree frog** (*Agalychnis callidryas*) lives high up in rainforest canopies in Central America. It is also known as the "monkey frog" because of its excellent climbing skills.

The **tree hole frog** (*Metaphrynella sundana*) is a native of lowland forests in Borneo. It lives in the hollows of tree trunks. The little frog uses tree hollows to amplify its mating calls so that it can be heard over long distances.

Who lives in a dry place? Many reptiles live in deserts. They can hide from the extreme temperatures in burrows. The desert is the last place you might expect to find an amphibian, but a few species have adapted to this extreme environment.

Who lives in a "house"? Some frogs have adapted to live in dead leaves that have fallen onto the forest floor whereas others cleverly use leaves to hide their eggs in until they hatch.

Who lives up in the trees? Most of the world's frogs live in tropical rainforests, where the temperature is nice and high and there is plenty of water.

Reptiles don't exist in Antarctica either. Unlike amphibians, they have watertight skin. This means that they don't dry out as quickly. Some reptiles live in hot, dry places such as deserts. Others live in warm swamps, rivers, or forests. A few have even adapted to a life at sea, but all return to land to lay their eggs.

All at SEA

The **yellow-bellied sea snake** (*Pelamis platurus*) has the largest lung of any snake. This helps it to control bouyancy so it can stay under water for long periods of time (up to three and a half hours).

The **hawksbill turtle** (*Eretmochelys imbricata*) uses its narrow beak to forage for mollusks, sponges, and other animals.

In the WET

The **African clawed frog** (*Xenopus laevis*) lives in ponds, lakes, or streams in southern Africa. It spends most of its time in water.

Northern water snake (*Nerodia sipedon*) lives in and around streams, ponds, lakes, and marshes. Water snakes are good swimmers. They have been known to herd tadpoles to the water's edge before tucking in.

Cool CREATURES

The **wood frog** (*Rana sylvatica*) survives freezing conditions by hibernating. It finds cracks in rocks, or gaps in logs, or can bury itself in leaves, to get through the cold winters.

Slow worm (*Anguis fragilis*) is a legless lizard that hibernates in piles of leaves, or in hollows between tree roots. It goes to sleep in October and emerges in March to breed in early summer.

Who's that in the sea? Amphibians can't cope with seawater because their skin is too thin to protect them from all the salt. Reptiles have thicker skin and a few species can regulate the salt in their blood and are therefore able to live in the sea.

Who likes to live somewhere moist? Amphibians provide tasty meals for many reptiles, so where they live you will often find reptiles, too. The Northern water snake lives near ponds, where it can catch amphibians.

Who's hiding from the cold? Some reptiles and amphibians live in temperate parts of the world, with cold winters. One of the ways in which they can survive these cold months is to save energy by hibernating.

Amazon horned FROG

Famed for its big appetite and its bad temper, the Amazon horned frog can grow to reach the size of a small dinner plate.

ENORMOUS GAPE

With a mouth that is wider than the length of its body, the Amazon horned frog can gobble up prey almost as big as itself.

Patient PREDATOR

Amazon horned frogs are voracious carnivores. They ambush their prey by sitting quietly and waiting for it to approach, before striking with a sudden snap of their jaws. **Amazon horned frogs aren't picky eaters.** Mostly they live on a diet of ants and other insects, but they will try to eat any animal smaller than themselves, including mice and, occasionally, rats. They don't always get it right, and may try to take on an animal that is too big for them to stomach.

Watch your feet! The Amazon horned frog will sometimes defend itself by attacking people if it is disturbed. They tend to grab anything that comes near them that could be edible.

Impressive **HORNS**

As its name suggests, the Amazon horned frog has big fleshy horns above its eyes. These are the largest horns of any of the horned frog species. These pointed brows help to disguise the frog's shape as it sits among the leaves on the forest floor awaiting its prey.

FROG FACTS

• Unlike other tadpoles, the Amazon horned frog tadpoles are **predatory** from the start. When they hatch, they attack other tadpoles and even attack each other.
• Females lay up to **1,000** eggs! They lay their eggs around aquatic plants.
• Males are **slightly smaller** than females. They make a mating call that sounds like a cow lowing (making a "moo" sound).

This frog grows up to 8 in (20 cm) in length.

How do crocodiles breathe underwater ?

Crocodiles have an amazing ability to breathe and hunt underwater at the same time. By closing a flap of skin at the back of their throats they prevent water from flowing into their lungs. They hold air in their lungs until they resurface. They are able to keep their mouths open to grab prey underwater, although they usually move to land to swallow it. **They also have flaps that can be closed over the nostril and ear openings.**

Saltwater crocodile
(Crocodylus porosus)

TURTLES

Aquatic turtles breathe through their lungs. The Florida softshell (right) has to surface and use its snout to fill its lungs with oxygen above water. Some turtles manage to stay underwater for weeks, living on very low oxygen levels.

Florida softshell turtle
(Apalone ferox)

Crocodiles can **waterproof their eyes** with a

FROGS

Frogs can breathe through their skin when they're in the water. Their skin absorbs oxygen from the water around them. Find out more about their amazing skin on pages 12–13.

Okinawa frog
(Rana sp.)

SEA SNAKES

Sea snakes can stay underwater for up to five hours. They have an enlarged lung that helps them to store lots of oxygen for when they're underwater. They have to resurface to breathe in more oxygen before they can make another dive.

Banded sea snake
(Laticauda colubrina)

CROCODILIANS have a FLAP of tissue behind the **tongue** *that covers* their **throats** when they are *submerged* in WATER.

membrane that acts as a **transparent shield**.

AMPHIBIANS and REPTILES have **different** ways of *bringing their young* into the world. Most hatch from an **egg.**

Amphibian eggs

A lot of amphibians lay their eggs in water, where they develop into tiny tadpoles.

However, many amphibians choose a sheltered egg-laying location where they guard their eggs or protect them in a layer of foam.

Other amphibians carry eggs on their backs, in their vocal sacs, in skin pockets, or even in their stomachs!

Reptile eggs

Most lizards lay eggs. They rarely return to their nests, although some skinks stay with their eggs to help maintain moisture and warmth.

Alligators and caimans make their nests from mounds of soil and leaves. Crocodiles and gavials lay their eggs in holes they dig in sand or dry, crumbly soil.

The shells of eggs laid by most turtles and tortoises are hard, but the shells of marine and river turtle eggs are softer.

Father FIGURES

In some species of frog, the father plays a key role. The male Darwin's frog takes care of the eggs as they develop. When the tadpoles hatch, he puts them in his vocal sac, where they grow until they are released as tiny frogs.

The male midwife toad (right) shows an interesting form of care. The female lays the eggs, but the male carries them on his legs! After about three weeks, the male takes the eggs to water, where the tadpoles hatch.

Absent PARENTS

The majority of geckos lay their eggs in bark or in the crevices of rocks. Geckos DO NOT take care of their young. The young are self-sufficient from birth. Turtles lay the most eggs out of all reptiles, but they don't watch over them. The eggs are left in soil or sand and when the baby turtles emerge, they are on their own. They have to learn survival skills pretty quickly!

When a caiman or alligator is born, it stays close to its mother. The young reptiles are protected by their mothers in the early weeks of their lives. When danger is detected they can use their mother as a shield by hiding under her body.

Boy or girl? The gender of baby crocodiles, turtles, and tortoises is often determined by egg temperature during incubation.

ACTUAL SIZE

from this..................................*to this!*

The GOLIATH FROG starts out SMALL.

Its **tadpole** is the same size as that of the

average frog, but it **keeps on**

growing until it reaches the *size of*

a cat. With legs outstretched, the *frog*

can MEASURE almost 3 ft (1 m) in length.

The goliath frog
(*Conraua goliath*)
lives in western Africa. It is found across a narrow range of Equatorial Guinea and Cameroon, in and around fast-flowing rivers and waterfalls. It is a popular food for locals.

Goliath frog
The goliath frog is the largest anuran (the class of animal that includes frogs and toads).

How small?
The smallest frog in the world is the Monte Iberia frog (*Eleutherodactylus iberia*) of Cuba. This tiny amphibian reaches a full size of only ⅓ in (9.8 mm) from snout to vent. It would sit comfortably on one of your fingernails.

Smallest frog
The Monte Iberia frog breeds by direct development, missing out the tadpole stage altogether.

SUN seekers

**Reptiles
are cold-blooded animals,** although once they have *sunbathed* their blood is about the same temperature as ours. Most reptiles live in **warm climates,** as they rely on their surroundings to obtain heat.

Reptiles keep their internal temperature at a constant level by moving to and from the shade.

A reptile can also obtain heat by resting its belly on a warm rock.

If the temperature doesn't suit a reptile then some

In the **summer months,** reptiles that live in tropical areas are *inactive* in the middle of the day, since it's too hot to move.

This graph shows the activity levels of a lizard. Take a look at how and where it spends its day.

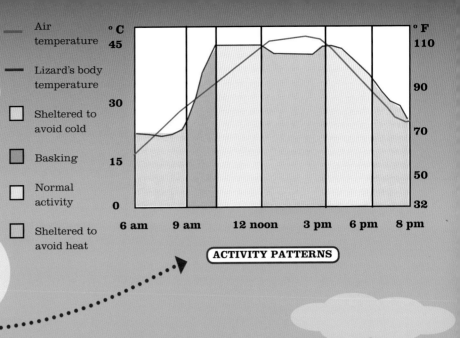

Air temperature

Lizard's body temperature

Sheltered to avoid cold

Basking

Normal activity

Sheltered to avoid heat

°C
45

30

15

0

°F
110

90

70

50

32

6 am   9 am   12 noon   3 pm   6 pm   8 pm

ACTIVITY PATTERNS

Reptiles need to stay warm when they eat. A snake that has eaten a meal but cannot get to a warm place might die if the food in its stomach is too cold to digest.

species will hibernate until the temperature is right.

Can you spot the FAKE?

FROGS use their MARKINGS for protection against *predators.* One of the frogs shown here has a cleverly positioned eyespot that *helps* it to confuse any potential ATTACKERS. Can you tell which one it is?

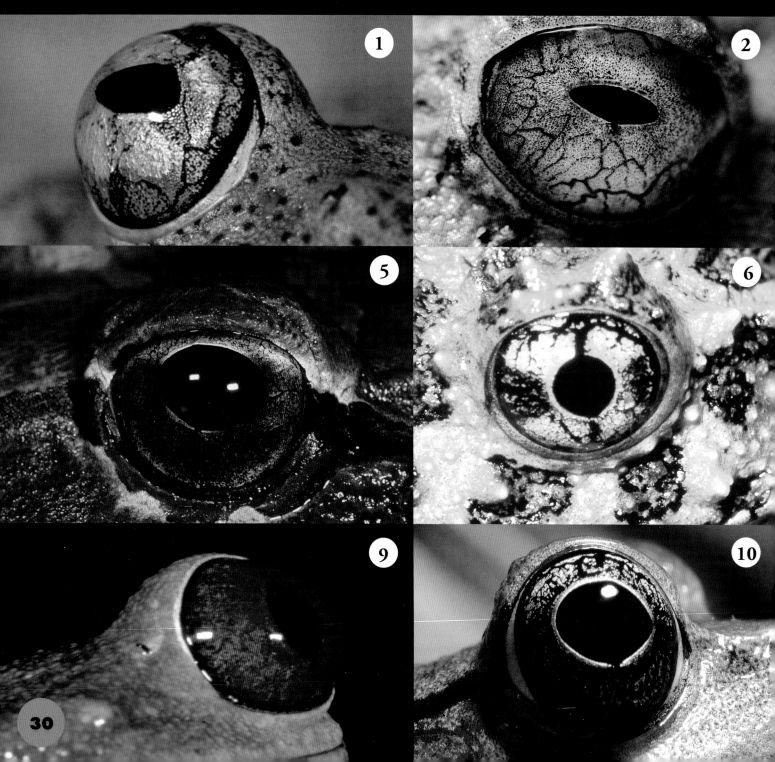